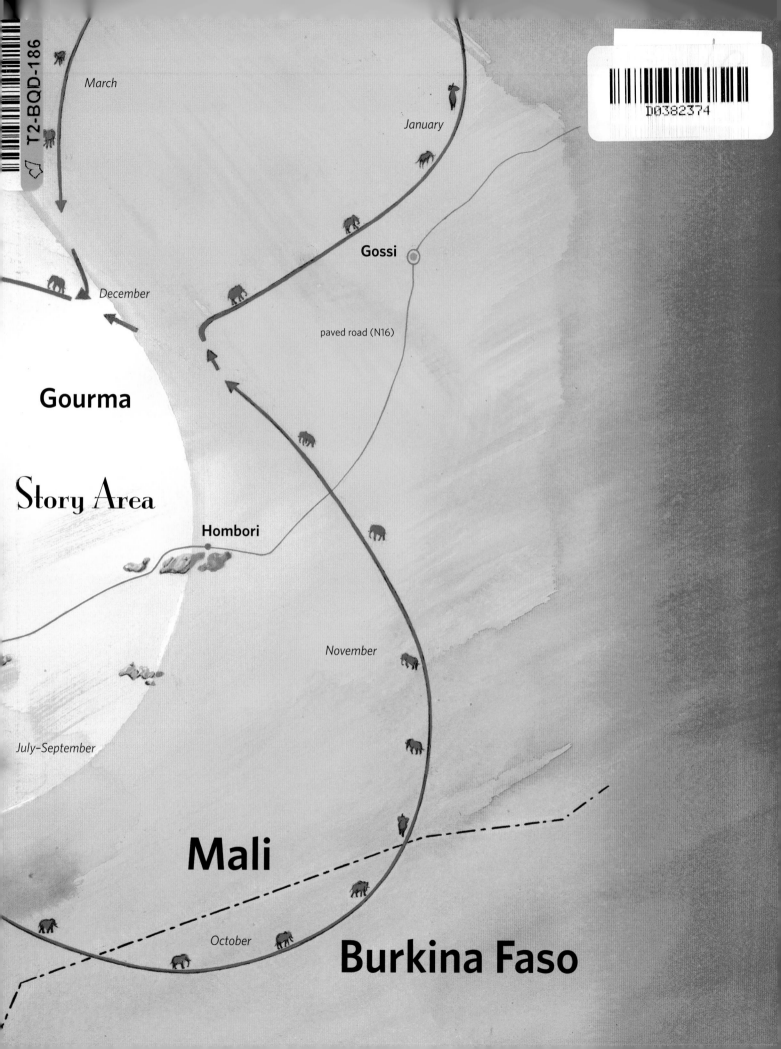

March

January

Gossi

December

paved road (N16)

Gourma

𝒮tory 𝒜rea

Hombori

November

July–September

Mali

October

Burkina Faso

Distributed in Canada by D&M Publishers, Inc.
Color separations by Embassy Graphics
Printed in May 2011 in China by South China Printing Co. Ltd.,
Dongguan City, Guangdong Province
Designed by Jay Colvin
First edition, 2011
1   3   5   7   9   10   8   6   4   2

www.fsgkidsbooks.com

Library of Congress Cataloging-in-Publication Data
Cowcher, Helen.
    Desert elephants / Helen Cowcher. — 1st ed.
        p.   cm.
    ISBN: 978-0-374-31774-4
    1. Elephants—Mali—Juvenile literature.   2. Elephants—Migration—Mali—Juvenile
literature.   3. Elephants—Effect of human beings on—Mali—Juvenile literature.
4. Desert ecology—Mali—Juvenile literature.   5. Human-animal relationships—Mali—
Juvenile literature.   6. Tuaregs—Mali—Juvenile literature.   7. Dogon (African people)—
Mali—Juvenile literature.   8. Fula (African people)—Mali—Juvenile literature.
9. Harmony (Philosophy)—Juvenile literature.   I. Title.

QL737.P98C69 2011
599.67'4096623—dc22

2010019817

HELEN COWCHER

DESERT ELEPHANTS

FARRAR STRAUS GIROUX / NEW YORK

In Mali, West Africa, the last remaining desert elephants follow the longest migration route of any elephant in the world. Their largest circular route is 300 miles long across harsh land just south of the Sahara desert. When the dry season begins, they start their journey for water. Their lives depend on it.

The Dogon, Fulani, and Tuareg peoples live in the same area as the elephants. On market days, people meet up and swap news. A Dogon girl stops to listen to the local desert radio outside the elephant ranger's office. Songs of ancient kingdoms stream out over the airwaves.

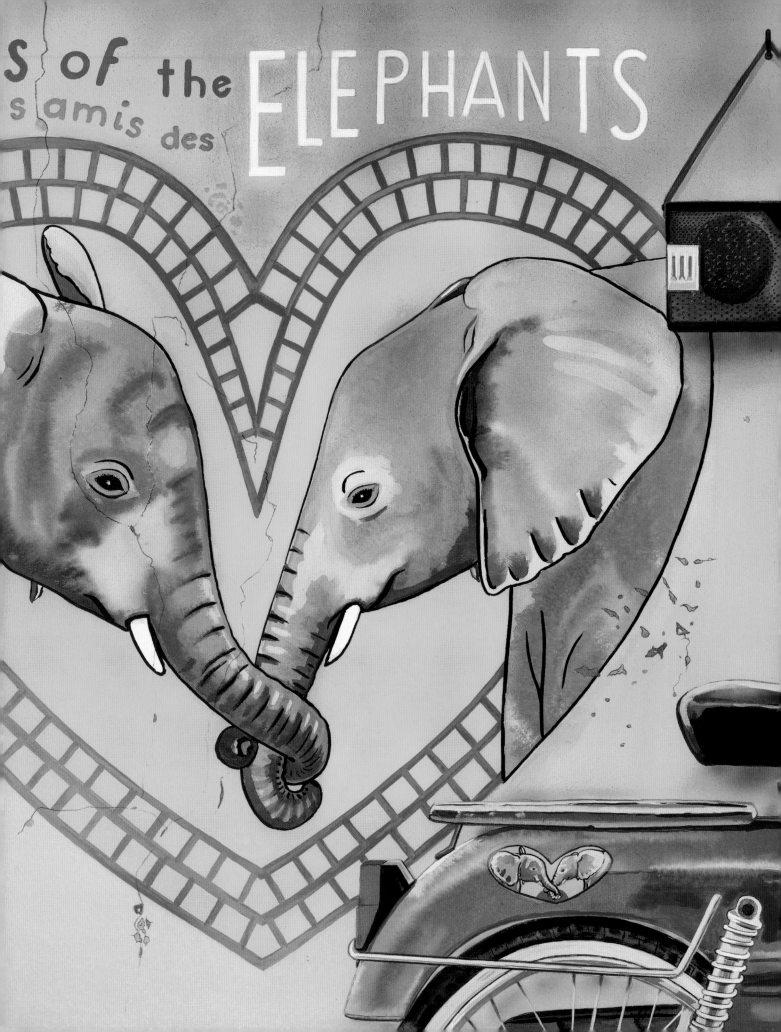

Now it is February, and far south of Timbuktu a group of elephants travel under cover of darkness. They are following their path in search of water to drink. No rain has fallen for four months, and the smaller pools are drying up.

The wise matriarch knows where to go.

They reach a small lake hidden within a forest. After they drink and eat, they sleep for a couple of hours in the very early morning.

That same morning, tourists come roaring across the sand. Their guide asks a Fulani herdsman, "What news of the elephants? Are they still nearby?"

"Oh yes, all around," he says.

The jeep speeds into the forest close to the lake . . .

Too close. Disturbed again! The sudden engine noise frightens the family groups. They trumpet in outrage. The Fulani say that elephants are becoming more aggressive— they worry that someone may get hurt.

That night in the forest, all is calm. Tuareg nomads have a saying: "We live with the elephants, and the elephants live with us." It has always been this way.

Talla, like the elephants, got water from the small lake among the trees. There is no other water for her to use. She loves to listen to the elephants' conversations in the gentle darkness beneath the stars.

One of the Tuareg's dogs likes to scamper back and forth toward the elephants. He is carefully tethered at dusk—otherwise he bothers the elephants and puts their whole camp at risk.

Many miles to the south, some newcomers have arrived near the
desert cliffs. They are not used to life with elephants and have built their
home on the pathway that leads to the "Elephants' Doorway."

In March, an elephant ranger visits. "It's unsafe for you to stay here,"
he warns them. "You are blocking the pathway."

"But how long has this pathway been here?"

"Oh, thousands of years!" he says. "Even before the great days of the Malian kingdoms."

"We didn't know. When will the elephants arrive?"

"The elephants will come when the rains begin in June. So there is still time to move."

"But where to?"

In a nearby village the chief hears of the newcomers' problem and calls a meeting of his elders under the palaver tree.

Desert radio plays in the background while the chief declares: "For elephants to follow their destiny, man has to be flexible. Our grandfathers told us that as long as elephants live here, our land will be healthy. We should help to keep the elephants' pathway clear. Shall we give a home to the strangers here?"

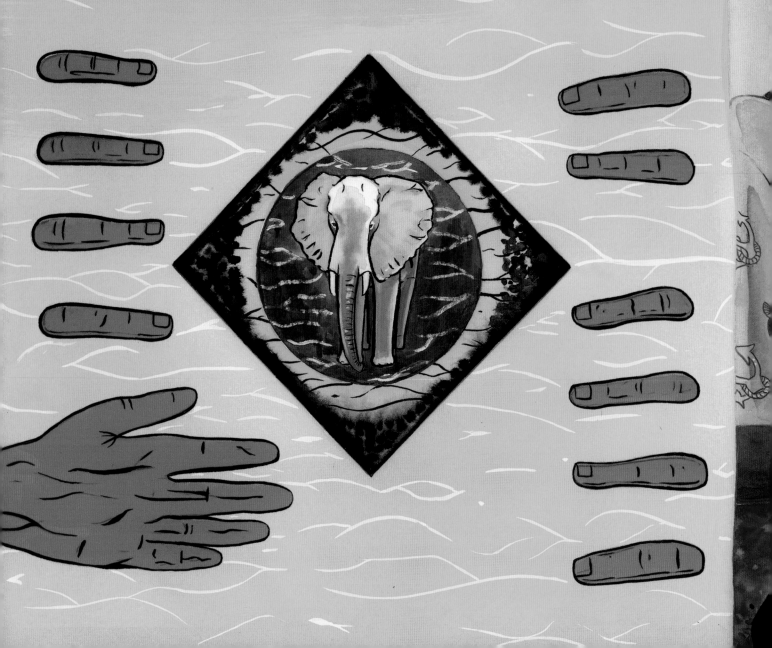

They hear a traditional saying on their local radio:
We know that each finger of the hand cannot work alone, but
when all the fingers come together our hands can do such work
it will be celebrated from Hombori to Timbuktu.
In the sizzling heat of April, an old village house is soon repaired so
that the strangers can join the villagers, out of harm's way.

Time passes.

Now, with the fiercest heat of June baking the ground, all the elephants have gathered to drink at the largest lake. The small lakes and pools have dried up, so this is the last place for them to get water before the time comes to march south.

Suddenly, the elephants sense rain!
From a long way off, their feet pick up seismic waves: thunder!
They make their way toward the water, swiftly, without stopping.

Through the night they go, arriving at dawn where a wall of rock lies ahead and there is only one path through the desert cliffs: the Elephants' Doorway.

Nothing can stop them now! Beyond, sweet, wet grass scents the air.

The elephants reach the flooded grassland and rush to drink, they are so thirsty. Then they plunge in and splash about in the wonderful water, and cool themselves in mud.

Back near the desert cliffs, people are happy, too. Now that the rainy season has begun, water flows deep in the village well. Yet these villagers know that the precious water will start drying up within a few months. Little by little, dust storms will darken their desert skies. The desert elephants and people live on shifting sands in a fragile land.

Author's Note

Who are the desert elephants?

These desert elephants are the last surviving 550 northernmost elephants in Africa and live mainly in an area called the Gourma in central Mali, West Africa. They used to travel as far north as Timbuktu, but because of human settlement they no longer go near the ancient city. There is a long tradition of peaceful coexistence between nomads and elephants in this region. Also, these elephants have not been hunted for ivory, partly because their tusks are much smaller, and of poorer quality, than those of other elephants.

Why were the elephants frightened by the tourists' vehicle?

In the past, the desert elephants were accustomed to camel trains: long lines of camels transporting salt and gold across the Sahara. But these elephants have never been used to vehicle noise. There is only one paved road (with little traffic) that traverses the elephants' land, and they only need to cross this road twice each year. Elephant rangers know quiet and safe ways to view elephants, who, as wild animals, naturally prefer to avoid man.

How can elephants sense rain falling a long way off?

Elephants can smell rain falling, and at greater distances they receive news of atmospheric conditions via infrasound. This is the same low-octave sound frequency with which whales signal to each other under the ocean. Elephants receive vibrations in their middle ear carried up through the body from their sensitive foot pads and trunk tips. Some people believe elephants can even pick up sound waves that travel through the earth from a large thunderstorm.

Why is finding water a problem for the elephants?

The elephants' habitat is part of the Sahel region, an arid zone that runs across Africa south of the Sahara desert. The temperature here is extremely hot. It can be 120°F (49°C). It rains for only four months a year. The small lakes in the northern Gourma gradually dry out as the year goes on. By May and early June, at the end of the dry season, there is only one lake that still has available water. The elephants must be there. An elephant and her calf will need 50 gallons of water a day to drink. During the wet season, late June through September, the elephants build up fat reserves while living in the south of their range. This helps them through the lean times in the north.

Who are the Dogon, Fulani, and Tuareg peoples?

The Dogon are from the southwestern plateau, which is an extension of the desert cliffs. They are traditionally gardeners and not herders. Tourists come to their rocky plateau to see their masked dances and beautiful hilltop architecture. The Fulani have herds of goats and cattle and travel with their animals, although many are settled. They live all over the Sahel region in different countries. The Tuareg live in northern Mali, Burkina Faso, Niger, Algeria, and elsewhere in the Sahara. They ride camels and live in tents with their families, moving from one watering place to the next. They are famed for producing fine leatherwork and jewelry. The Dogon have their own ancient religion, whereas the Tuareg and Fulani follow Islam.

Why is the local desert radio important?

People in Mali are used to hearing many languages, but about 70 percent cannot read or write. Radio is an important way of communicating and letting people know what is going on in the outside world. Radio stations advise about legal rights concerning many things, like the cutting and planting of native trees. The radio tells people about how to protect the land they share with the elephants, gives them advice on health and education, and broadcasts programs about women's issues. People can also relay personal messages via radio. For example, if the men lose animals in the huge areas between settlements, the radio will send out a message so other herders can help pass this information along. It is in everyone's interest to help one another. Radios also play soap operas and music.

What is the significance of the pictures printed on some African fabrics?

These dramatic textiles are another way of communicating. Designs can include popular goods like fans, phones, stoves, or water pumps, or more traditional symbols like hands, fingers, or eyes. They can also provide publicity for social campaigns. Still produced in the Netherlands, Dutch wax prints are also made in many African countries, such as Mali, Ghana, Senegal, and Burkina Faso. Dutch wax fabric can also come from China.

Why talk under the palaver tree?

"Palaver" is not the name of a tree. A "palaver" is a conference or discussion and, in Africa, the place in the shade of a large tree where the village chief and elders may sort out disputes and discuss plans. Those who are not good speakers can ask a spokesperson to present points on their behalf. Discussions can go on for hours, until eventually a decision is reached.

Useful Web sites:
www.sahel.org.uk
www.wild.org

Acknowledgments

The author wishes to give special thanks to her consultants in the United Kingdom: Dr. Susan Canney, Department of Zoology, Oxford University, England, and Dr. Mary Myers, specialist in development communications and radio in Africa; in the United States: Mr. Vance Martin, president of WILD Foundation, Boulder, Colorado; in Mali: elephant expert Mr. El Mehdi Doumbia of the Antenne des Eaux et Forêts, Gossi, Gourma. Thanks also to Radio Daande Douentza and to Ms. Mary Allen Ballo of Sahel ECO.

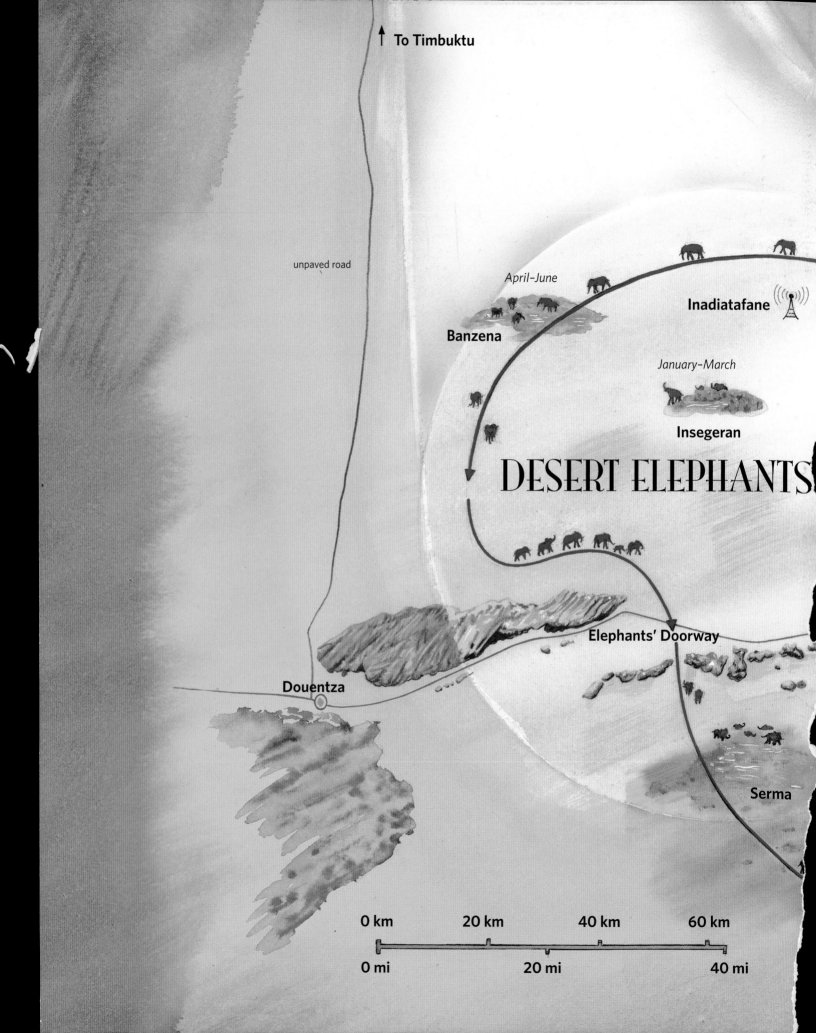

↑ **To Timbuktu**

unpaved road

April–June

Inadiatafane

Banzena

January–March

Insegeran

DESERT ELEPHANTS

Elephants' Doorway

Douentza

Serma

| 0 km | 20 km | 40 km | 60 km |

| 0 mi | 20 mi | 40 mi |